Brew Your Own Beer

Impress friends by knowing all about beer and brewing it yourself

AMARPREET SINGH

Publisher - The Thought Flame

THE THOUGHT FLAME
TURNING SPARK INTO FLAME

info@thethoughtflame.com

www.thethoughtflame.com

Table of Contents

Introduction

Do you find yourself suddenly want to make you own beer at home? Have you ever brewed beer in your home before? Or are you all new to all of this? You would not be the first one.

In fact many people, do to the economy nowadays find that it is just cheaper to make their own beer at home rather than going to a bar. Aside from saving money on a large bar tab, home brewing your own beer is a great hobby to enjoy. The best part about it is that doing it does not require a huge investment on your part in regards to both time and money. Home brewing can be done with little money and little time needed and it is a great way to impress your friends with your new hobby and skill.

In this eBook you will learn a variety of different cool tips and tricks such as how to make your own beer at home in easy to follow steps that any person can easily follow, how you can save money on all of the supplies you need, what supplies are recommended for home brewing and where you can get them at a cheap price, and special techniques you can use to make the homebrewing process easier. I hope you enjoy this eBook and above all learn the right way on how to make your own home brewed beer.

Chapter One: 16 Tips To Follow Before You Get Started

Now before you can start brewing and enjoying your home brewed beer, there are a few tips I would like to offer you so that you can enjoy this hobby for as long as you pursue it. In this chapter we will discuss what these tips are in detail and helpful insight on what you can do to follow these tips.

1. Talk With Experienced Homebrewers-the science of making your own beer at home is a hobby that can be learned by anyone that has a willingness to learn how to do it. There are many people who enjoy this hobby and have been building their craft for many years. These are people you want to get in touch with and that can

help you out if you ever find yourself in a jam. Join as many beer forums as you can and learn from ones that have the years of knowledge necessary to help you out.

As a tip make sure you do not follow the directions on any ingredient labels that you come across. Some of the instructions you will find are weird and can have a negative effect on the outcome of your beer. Make sure that before you start mixing ingredients together that you know what you are doing and if you have any questions, do not hesitate to jump on your forum and ask an experience beer homebrewer.

2. Try To Watch Some In Action Beforehand-The best way to learn how to make your own beer at home is to watch someone do it themselves before you give it a try. The best way to learn is to watch someone actually brew the beer first and then bottle it so that you can follow exactly what they did to the T. Once you watch it firsthand, you

will feel confident that you can do the same and come up with the same result. If you don't know anybody who actually brews their own beer, just hop on Google and YouTube and watch as many videos and tutorials as possible.

3. Try To Get A Second Opinion-Do not feel embarrassed or silly for asking for help. Even the best of us need a helping hand sometimes and as I said before, the best way to learn is to learn from people who have experience. Every experienced brewer started out as a newbie at some point or another and knew nothing of the process in the beginning. Remember if you have any doubts about anything you are doing whether you are in the brewing process or in the bottling process, don't be afraid to reach out for help.

If you find yourself having a ton of question, search the Internet, look on different homebrewing forums or ask other homebrewers.

Most of the time these people are most than willing and happy to help newcomers out. Keep in mind that a majority of the time, you will get different answers from the different people you ask as these people use their own methods to homebrew their beer. However, by asking a lot of people you will get a general idea of what to do and that you know will work for you.

4. Online vs. Local-while there are a variety of advantages to ordering the supplies you need in order to brew your beer at home, you will still need to find a local supply store where you can find all of your supplies. Often times you will need to both taste and smell many of the ingredients that you will not be able to do that if you purchase them online. You will need to find a place where you can see the different ingredients firsthand.

You will also need to find a place where you can get ingredients in an emergency situations or ingredients that you may randomly need. The advantage to finding a local store to get your supplies from is that you have the option of talking to people experienced in the home brewing field. If you do not know where to find a local home brewing store just go on to Google and find your local homebrew club and ask some of the members if they have a place they can recommend.

5. Realize That Homebrewing Requires Lots of Cleaning-if you are going to be brewing your own beer at home, you need to realize the amount of cleaning that goes into it. You will essentially become a janitor in your home as you will be cleaning, sanitizing and cleaning up after the brewing process for about ninety percent of the time. If you are not committed into putting in the

time and effort required to homebrew correctly, then maybe it is time you begin looking for a new hobby.

6. Organize Yourself-Before you begin to brew, organize all of your materials and ingredients so they are readily available when you need them. It is helpful to create a checklist where you can list of the ingredients and supplies you will need for a certain bath and even create a time schedule where you can ensure that you follow every step you need to in order to make your beer in a timely and effective manner. By planning and prepping before you begin to brew, it will save you from going crazy when you can't find something you need right at the moment you need it. Another advantage to organizing is that you will make the whole operation of brewing much simpler and will help yourself to be much more relaxed, so that you can have more fun in the long run.

7. Take Your Time-When it comes to brewing your beer from home, the key thing to do is to take your time. By rushing around like a chicken with its head cut off you can accidentally drop something or miss a step in the brewing process. By rushing you risk the overall outcome of your finished product and risk consuming more of your time fixing whatever accidents you make when it could have been prevented beforehand.

8. Test Other Beers Before Hand-make a point to get out there a try a variety of home brewed beers or commercial beers that you can find. This will help raise your own confidence in your overall success for your first brewing project and will also help you to understand what elements of beer you like so you can recreate it in your own batch.

9. Start Off Slow -There is no need to buy thousands of dollars worth of brewing supplies or ingredients when you are a first time brewer. Easily start with a simple starter kit that costs no more than $200 and take the time to experiment for a while. While you learn you are going to make mistakes and learn from the mistakes you make. This will help you to become a more experienced brewer. As time passes you will know for yourself when you need to upgrade your supplies and when that time comes you will understand the value of the overall upgrade and appreciate it in the long run.

10. Experiment-Do not be afraid to experiment as much as you can when you homebrew. This is the point of this hobby, to build on your experience and to increase your understanding of the homebrewing process. Try to use different yeast products from time to time, use different kinds of

hops, change the grain you use and try as many flavors of beer as possible.

11. Don't Ask Other People For Their Opinion On Recipes-the reason as to why this is important is because simply put, if a brewer hasn't tasted or made a recipe for themselves, they won't know whether or not the recipe is good. How can this help you? What you need to do is experiment for yourself and see how your own beer comes out. Sometimes you will make some really great brews, other times you may not. Continue to experiment until you find the recipe that is an instant success for you.

12. Don't Stress Yourself Over Minor Details-there is no need to stress yourself over minor details or problems that will not do anything for you but give you a migraine. If the temperature of your

brew is off by a degree or two, don't worry about it. The only thing that you need to worry about is making sure that your primary sugar is measured accurately. You need to worry that you do not add too much or too little as both results can affect the outcome of your brew.

Remember, home brewing is supposed to be a hobby, not a stressful pastime.

13. Whatever You Do, Don't Throw Out your Batch-if you realized that you messed up on your brew or that you accidentally tossed in the wrong ingredient, don't throw out the batch without trying it first. By doing this you pretty much throw your money away which is as bad as if you bought all of your supplies and did nothing with them. Even if you taste the beer and it is not what you were looking for, don't throw it away. Ferment it, bottle it and bottle it. Give it time to age a bit before trying it again. These crucial

stages can affect and improve the beer, but only if you give it time to do so.

14. Don't Expect To Be Perfect-by taking the risk of knowing that you may fail at some point or another while you brew for the first time, you will be able to become a master homebrewer in no time. Brewing at home includes taking risk, especially risking to fail at one point or another, but this will help you to learn as you go and even have the chance of brewing something fantastic on accident. You need to accept the fact that at some point you may have to throw out a brew or two. What you need to remember here is to relax and not to be too hard on yourself. Take great notes and learn from any mistakes that you may make.

15. Above All Else Have Fun-you cannot take the hobby of homebrewing too seriously. As it was stated before the whole point of this hobby is for

you to have done doing something that is creative and that will help to impress your friends. Don't become too focused on the small details such as cleaning, recipes, time charts and waiting out the fermentation process. You need to remember that you started homebrewing to essential have fun doing it. You need to learn as you go with homebrewing and you need to keep in mind that you will not make the perfect batch on your first try. You may need many tries in order to become a proficient brew master and to find the batch that stuns everyone who tries it.

If you are a perfectionist then do your best to learn all that there is to learn about the homebrewing process so that you can have fun in the long run. Take the time to learn about the different yeasts you can use, the different grains and hops that work well with each other and what flavors blend together well to make a delicious batch.

When you homebrew, the point is to have fun doing something that you enjoy. Have fun showing off your skills and your knowledge about the homebrewing process and you will find out how much fun you can truly have by having a worthwhile hobby to commit to.

16. RELAX-you simply cannot overwhelm yourself with making the best homebrewing batch you can make. If you do you will simply not have fun taking part in this hobby. Remember, you will make a mistake at some point and you need to take whatever happens with a grain of salt. The more mistakes you make, the more of a chance you have to produce a decent and delicious beer in the end. Remember, all you are doing is making beer. You are not conducting brain surgery.

Chapter Two: How To Begin Homebrewing and What Supplies You Will Need

Before you can start brewing your own beer from home, there are a few essential things that you need and you need to know how you can start. In this chapter of this eBook you will learn exactly what supplies you need in order to begin brewing your own beer from your home, how to get those supplies at a cheap price and what steps are that need to be taken step-by-step in the brewing process.

What Supplies You Will Need

Now remember, when you start out be aware that you may suddenly want to buy the highest quality equipment that you think you will need. You need to stop yourself right then and there. When you start out you don't need to rush out and waste all of your money to buy the latest top of the line products to begin brewing your beer from home. Start small and only once you gain enough experience then go out and slowly buy more expensive equipment that will help make the brewing process better. Here are a list of item that you will need to make sure is in your arsenal of home brewing equipment.

1. A Large Boiling Kettle-this is essential as this is where the brewing process will take place. Try to get at least a three gallon pot to use as a boiler and later on upgrade to a 5 gallon boiling kettle so that you can make large batches of your beer. Then lastly you can upgrade to a mighty 9 gallon boiling kettle to make as many batches of your beer as you want. By using a three gallon boiling kettle at first, remember it will allow you to make

a three gallon batch of your beer that you will need to boil first.

Remember, when you boil your batch first the cause of it is for the beer to become caramelized and to darken its original color. The more batches you boil, the better your ending product will be. However, the more space that you have in the boiling process cuts down on the risk of having potential boil overs and wasting of your batch. Of course you can prevent such small accidents by standing vigilant and ensuring that you constantly stir your batch to prevent it from overflowing and possible scorching.

Also by investing in an even larger pot to boiling your brews helps you to add in extra water so that you don't get disgusted when you have to pour the nasty wort into your fermenter.

When it comes to finding the best boiling kettle to use for your brewing needs, it is highly recommended to look for those with features that will be useful. Try to find a boiling kettle that has a valve spigot as it will come in handy during time where you need one. Some other features you can look for in your boiling kettle are built-in thermometers, diverter plates, false bottoms and sight glass tubes to help you measuring the liquid volume.

2. Fermentors-the kind of fermentors that I recommend finding to help best fit your specific needs is glass carboy fermentors. The reason as to why I recommend this specific type of fermentors is because they are much easier to clean and sanitize than popular plastic fermenters that are used.

There are many advantages to using glass carboy fermentors such as less prone to common leaks often found in plastic fermenters, less chance of having nicks or scratches in the fermentor and they are sealed more reliably than the plastic ones. If you take the chance on getting a plastic fermenter, you will soon regret it.

3. Choosing Buckets and/or Carboys-when it comes to choosing the right bucket or carboy for your fermentor it is important to go with your instinct and pick the one that will best fit your needs. While most buckets and carboys on the market today offer some headspace available to excess fermentation foam, many others do not. If you are reluctant to use a certain bucket or carboy, test it out for yourself first by testing their capacity before using it for yourself to brew a batch or your own beer.

If you choose to use plastic buckets or carboys, make sure that it is food grade plastic to ensure safety and keep in mind that if you plan on storing the beer for longer than a month, you should avoid using it completely. The disadvantage of using plastic over glass is that your beer may contain off flavors after a few months as this is due to the plastic's overall permeability.

However, know this, that while a few homebrewers have no problem using glass carboys, a majority of them hate them and for good reason. Glass carboys are too heavy for the average person to handle, they are slick to the touch and they can create one hell of a mess if dropped accidentally. Either way, go with your gut and pick the best carboy that you need to accommodate your needs.

4. Steel Spoon-if you plan on becoming the next homebrewing master, you need to equip a strong, long steel spoon in your brewing arsenal. The reason why your spoon needs to be strong is because it needs to stand up to the task of stirring through sticky and thick mashes of beer and needs to be able to create whirlpools of boiling

wort. The reason why your steel spoon will need to be long is because it needs to be able to reach the very bottom of your boiling kettle without having your fingers touch the wort and risk burning yourself. The last reason as to why your spoon needs to be steel is because if you decide to choose a plastic or wood spoon, both can prove to be very flimsy and almost impossible to sanitize.

5. Thermometers-a thermometer is probably the most important piece of equipment that you will use during your homebrewing operation. I recommend using a stick on thermometer as this will help you to monitor the temperature of your overall ferment and will help let you know when you can top off your recipe.

Whatever you do, do not use thermometers that contain mercury! The glass of these kinds of thermometers is very fragile and the mercury itself is very poisonous to humans. The best kind of thermometer that you can use for your operation is a bi-metal thermometer, a digital stick thermometer, or a digital probe thermometer. Either way make sure that you check the accuracy of whatever thermometer you choose to use by comparing it to another accurate thermometer that you have. You can easily test it by using boiling water.

6. Outdoor Propane Burner-

investing in an outdoor propane burner will save you money in the long run as it will save you on energy and will be more effective use on your bathes than an electric burner. Other advantages to using an outdoor propane burner is that it not only do you have more control over the temperature you need to boil your batch, but you can boil your batch much faster and you can clean up after much easier.

If you have a spouse who prefers that you keep your brewing operation remains in a place that is far away from the kitchen, an outdoor propane burner will help to make that person happy and help to keep the mess out of your home. However, if you live in an apartment, the option of choosing this kind of burner is not for you.

The thing to remember here is that if you decide to use this kind of burner, try to keep a fire extinguisher handy in the case of a sudden emergency.

7. A Timer-if you are not the type of person that wants to stand over a boiling kettle for over an hour to make sure that you take it off the flame, I recommend that you get a timer that you can easily carry with you. While it is best to stand near your boil to prevent accidental scorching or to prevent boil-overs, a timer will help you to keep track of how long you boil your brew for. A

timer will prove especially helpful if you decide give all-grain brewing a try.

8. Auto-Siphon-if you find yourself having trouble siphoning your beer, you should consider purchasing an auto-siphon. You can find these virtually in any home brewing supply store or online supply store and it is a product that works great. I recommend that when you buy an auto-siphon buy one that reaches approximately 4 feet in length and made of food grade tubing.

9. Hydrometers-the hydrometer is yet another important piece of equipment that you need for the homebrewing process. However, they are made of ultra thin glass and tend to break very easily so it is best that you get a second one as an emergency backup.

You can also purchase a specially designed hydrometer that is perfect for those who don't want to waste their time figuring out what the alcohol content of their beer is. They are very easy to read and handy to have around, but it is important that you check the alcohol content scale to gauge how strong or weak your beer is.

How To Homebrew Your Beer Step-By-Step

Brewing your own beer from home is a simple, yet complicated process. Below are simple step-by-step instructions on how to brew your own beer and what process each step contains.

1. Brew The Beer-you will boil both malt extract and hops together with approximately 3-9 gallons of water. This process will take about an

hour and during this time it will help to sterilize the malt extract and release the inner flavor qualities of the hops.

Normally the grains that you use are steeped into the malt and hops extract prior to boiling. This helps to add more flavor and coloring to your batch at the end of the process.

2. Cooling and Fermenting Your Batch-once your brew has been boiled for an hour, it is now called a wort. The wort must then be cooled to room temperature and then siphoned out of the pot to be placed in the fermentor. Here it is mixed with more water to achieve the size of the boiling kettle you received. Once the wort and water mixture reaches room temperature the next thing that you have to do is add yeast to help start the fermentation process.

Here you need to remember to keep everything sanitized and clean. If you don't you risk bacteria infecting your batch and then having to toss it out before you can even finish making it. You can use the anti lock feature to keep the pot sealed during the process. This process will take approximately 1 to 2 weeks to ferment successfully.

3. Prime and Bottle Your Batch-at the end of the fermentation process, you can begin to bottle your new beer. You need to siphon it out into a clean separate container to prepare to put it into your bottles. In the container you will then need to add any sugar or cornstarch you need and mix it thoroughly. Next you will need to siphon out the beer and into the bottles you have and then cap it securely with a bottle-capping product. This will help to ensure no air can enter your bottle and cause the beer to become stale.

4. Age Your Beer-Once you have placed your new beer into your bottles, you need to then age it for

approximately 2 to 6 weeks. During this stage in the homebrewing process the yeast that you mixed into your batch will help to ferment the sugar you added in the last step, helping to create carbon monoxide.

Carbon Monoxide is essential, as it will help to carbonate your beer and make bubbly. This will also help to remove excess proteins and yeast that you don't need and help to enhance the overall flavor of your beer. One thing to keep in mind is that your beer will need to age for months at a time in order to reach the exact flavor that you want, though you can usually begin drinking it after a month of aging it

5. Drink It Up!-Once your beer has reached the right aging time, all that is left for you to do is to put your bottles in the fridge and drink it up when you are ready. You will soon realize how great your own homemade beer will taste.

Of course this step will differ from person to person and of course the process may take longer for some people than it does for others. Overall it should take a few hours to complete and the fermentation and aging process will take a few weeks to complete. Look to commit about 4 hours of time to boil and bottle while the aging and fermentation will take approximately 4 weeks until your beer is drinkable. If you are the type of person who loves things that are made from scratch then you will find this hobby to be enjoyable especially if you live a busy and chaotic life.

Chapter Three: All About Hops and Yeast

Hops are one of the most important ingredient besides yeast that you will use when you brew your own beer in your home. This chapter is dedicated to everything you will need to know about hops and what helpful tips you will need in order to make your beer the best that it can be. We will also cover the importance of yeast and how it can alter the end result of your homebrewed beer.

What Are Hops?

Experienced brewers and beer enthusiasts often describe the flavor of beer by saying things such as it is hoppy or the beer didn't use a lot of hops. But what are they exactly? Hops are one of the basic and most important ingredients one will use in the beer brewing process. Hops is actually part of the hop plant which surprisingly apart of the hemp family.

Flavor wise hops contains an oil that every beer needs and that give beer its bitter flavor. However, this flavor is what helps to create a well-balanced beer and which acts as a natural beer preservative.

Helpful Tips About Hops

1. Use Hop Pellets Instead of Whole Hops-when you use hop pellets instead of whole hops, they work just as well and in fact help to create less of a mess. This pellets are made from dried hops and are the result of the dried hops being pressed into a concentrated form. This concentrated form

is what helps to give hops their bitter taste. One thing to keep in mind is due to their concentrated state hop pellets are natural 15% more bitter than whole hops so make sure that you adjust your batch recipe accordingly and make sure that you do not add too much to your batch.

2. Pay Attention To The Alpha Rating-if you do not know what the alpha rating is, it is the rating used to describe how bitter certain hops are and it is what experienced homebrewers use to gauge how bitter they want their own batches to be. The best tip that I can give you is that if you wish to reduce the amount of bitterness that your hops contain, refrigerate them or even freeze them.

Also keep in mind to keep your hops fresh as this too will lower their overall bitterness. Try to keep your hops is a air tight bag and if you can even vacuum seal them, that will be better.

Also keep in mind that the longer you hold on to your hops, the less bitter they will be. It has been proven that hops will drop from a 5% Alpha rating to a 4% alpha rating if they are kept longer than 6 months in storage. So the thing to take away here is to use your hops in a time effective manner before they lose their bitterness.

3. Buy Your Hops In Bulk-it is no secret that it is best to keep your hops as fresh as you can in order to make a better tasting beer, you can save more money in the long run by buying as many hops as possible. To find the best deals look for a supply store online. Now by bulk I don't mean go out and buy 20 pounds of hops at this very moment. What I mean is get a few ounces. Once you get them refrigerate them as soon as possible and keep them in a tight sealed container. The sooner you can use the hops the better so make sure that you check their shelf-life and sell-by

date in order to ensure that you use them by that time.

4. Don't Be Afraid to Try Different Hops-don't be afraid to try using a variety of different hops. Hops differ in taste and by experiment with different hops you can eventually find the perfect mixture and bitterness that will help make your beer taste amazing. Experiment with the different quantities and varieties of hops and remember to take note of the hops your like and dislike. Also keep note of your mistakes and your success so you can reproduce those results.

5. Attempt To Grow Your Own Hops-there is nothing better than using an ingredient that you grow from scratch to make your own beer from scratch. Hops grow back every year so you only need to plant the seeds of the flower once, so the plus side is that if you can take care of the plant, you can use it for many years to come. Hops

come from plant that needs water, plenty of sun and fertile soil in order for it to thrive and produce the highest quality hops you will find.

If growing your own hops is something that you are interested in start by growing your plant using the roots from females hops plants and within a couple of weeks you will begin to see new hops flowers growing. Also try to grow different varieties of the flower to learn for yourself what kind of conditions your hops plant best thrives in.

The Importance of Yeast

Yeast is one of the important ingredients you will use in your home brewed beer, aside from hops. It serves the most important function which is to break down the sugar you add in you freshly brewed batch and to help create carbon monoxide to help give your beer the carbonation that most beer enthusiast desire. Often times people forget how important yeast is in the beer brewing process even though it help to add more flavoring and coloring into your beer once it is ready to be drunk by you. In this section we will cover the most mistakes new homebrewers make with yeast and what some helpful tips are so you can get the most out of your beer.

Common Mistakes New Homebrewers Make

One of the most complicated ingredients that new homebrewers cannot get a handle on is yeast and bacteria. New homebrewers tend to follow every step correctly in the homebrewing process, yet forget the importance of how yeast affects the overall quality of their beer. The end result will end up being a poor tasting beer that will likely get dumped down the drain. Below are some common mistake new homebrewers tend to make when it comes to the yeast process and are what you should avoid if you wish to make a great tasting beer.

1. Overcomplicated the Yeast Adding Process-one of the many things that new homebrewers are known for is their ability to overcomplicate a very simple process. They over think it and this over thinking can lead to disastrous results. The key to remember here is to research before hand everything you can about yeast beforehand, so that it will not affect the overall quality of your beer. By doing this new brewers can help yield more successful results and will ultimately continue making great tasting beer with every batch.

Another thing that new brewers should do is to follow their instinct. Everywhere online whether you are looking at homebrewing websites or have joined a home brewing forum, many people will give different advice on what type of yeast you should use and almost always they will report different results. Go with your instinct and experiment for yourself so that you can find the best yeast that will help make your beer taste great in the end.

2. Forgetting To Control Their Fermentation Temperature-another common mistake that Homebrewers make is forgetting to control their fermentation temperature. The temperature in the fermentation process is one of the most important variables in home brewing and can lead to disastrous results if it is not done correctly. Yeast has a whole will only be activated at a certain temperature so if you have the temperature too low or too high, the yeast will not activate when it needs to.

The temperature during the fermentation process will differ from batch to batch so that is something new homebrewers need to keep in mind. For example is you want to make an American ale, the temperature during the fermentation process will need to be kept between 67 and 73 degrees in order for the yeast to activate.

During the fermentation process, the temperature should be kept at a level temperature throughout the entire process. What I recommend is choosing a special place to keep your batch where you know the temperature itself will not fluctuate and continue to use that spot for every batch that you make.

3. Make Too Many Changes-as a new brewer you may tend to want to change nearly every step you do right after your first batch. My advice here is to take it slow. There is no need to rush and

rushing or changing things will only affect the outcome of your beer and leave you with something that tastes disgusting. I recommend perfecting your process first before you try to change certain steps or certain ingredients.

There is no question if you will make mistakes; the question is when will you make those mistakes. Mistakes are what is going to help you to perfect your own process of brewing and that will help to make you a more experienced homebrewer over time.

Tips To Follow With Yeast

1. Try Using Dry Yeast-using dry yeast is probably the most simple and cost effective type of yeast to use than liquid yeast for beginners. However, if you plan on using dry yeast the most important thing that you will have to do with it is to

rehydrate it. If a recipe asks you to sprinkle the dry yeast onto your wort, DO NOT DO IT! What you need to do is first boil one pint of water before you prepare the wort and sprinkle the yeast into the water before mixing it into the wort. You need to do this simply because it can only be activated at a temperature between 95-105 degrees. If the water is too hot or too cold will not help it to activate to help age and ferment your batch.

If you want to a higher quality and fresher batch of beer, then use liquid yeast as it will give you the results you desire. As yeast is one of the most important ingredients you will use to make your beer, it is not something you want to cut corners or skimp on. The most you will spend on liquid yeast is approximately $5 to $6 extra, but the results it can garnish are well worth the investment.

As a helpful tip try to spend a few minutes before you plan to brew and make a starter bottle using the liquid yeast and allow it to ferment a few days before you begin the brewing process. This will help to make the fermentation process go by faster and will help to deliver you an amazing and great tasting beer.

In the long run you will save more money on liquid yeast then you will on dry yeast as you can make it stretch further by re-using it at least 4 to 5 times. The way you can reuse it is to siphon your batch into the primary fermentor, pour it into a bottling bucket or second fermentor, harvest the liquid yeast from the bottom of the fermentor and then use it in your next batch.

Once you have used your yeast as many times as you can, label the slutty with the date it was first used and record what type of yeast was used. You want to do this because you can use the slurry to make a yeast starter.

In order to figure out what kind of yeast is the best for you to use, test out different types of yeast in two separate fermenters for each batch that you make. That way you can produce different flavors of beer while still using the same ingredients. Make sure to record your experiments and note your results so that you can recreate them in the future.

2. Make Your Yeast Starter-by making your own yeast starter, you will effectively help to start a more rigorous and fast starting fermentation process. In order to create your own yeast starter all you need to do is begin mixing one ounce of your malt extract and one pint of water then pour it into a sterilized bottle. Next make sure that you cover the bottle with either plastic wrap or tin foil. Once your wort has cooled down to the sixty to seventy degree mark add your yeast and shake it up to combine it. Re-cover it and make sure to let

it sit out in room temperature for a minimum of four days. During that time to gently mix it up from time to time to make sure the yeast is activated and mixing with the other contents.

The reason as to why you want to make a yeast starter is because this will give you a chance to help the yeast multiply quickly and gain strength, so that the fermentation process of your batch goes smoothly. Once you use the starter, the fermentation will set off rather quickly to the point it will surprise you.

If you need other ways to make a yeast starter, simply pour some of your wort into a muffin tin, freeze it and then put the iced wort into a few Ziploc bags. Store them in your freezer until you are ready to boil them. Cool them after boiling and then add in your yeast starter. If you are planning to make a higher gravity beer, than you will need to use more than one quarter of a yeast starter. To do this prepare a normal amount of the starter and then add between four to ten pints of the wort so that you can use it the next day. This will help the yeast to grow due to the fact that is given much larger room to grow.

Chapter Four: The Fermentation and Bottling Process

The word fermentation simply means when the wort you made finally become beer through a complicated and complex conversion of different sugars when is converted into both alcohol and carbon dioxide. Yeast is what helps to complete the conversion as it essentially eats the sugars. Your primary job is to provide the yeast with the right conditions so it can effectively do its job. Fermentation itself can take anywhere from 2 to 3 weeks to complete. For fermentation to take place all that needs to be done you need to leave your batch in the vat for at least two to three weeks and you need to leave it there even if it appears that they the fermentation process seems to be complete.

The way that you can tell if the fermentation is complete all that you need to do is take a few gravity readings every couple of days. If the gravity readings are consistent every couple of days, then your beer has been fermented completely. Some experienced homebrewers use the knowledge of inactive airlock activity as an indication that the fermentation process is complete. If you are still unsure that your beer is complete you can easily use a hydrometer to make sure.

To conduct the fermentation process simply complete the steps below:

The Fermentation Process

1. Use Vodka Instead of Water-Instead of using water to put in your airlock or bubbler, use vodka. Vodka will help to kill any microbes or harmful

bacteria that may affect your batch before it can finish fermenting. By using vodka you also get a small bonus in your beer by adding a little more alcohol to it.

2. Be Prepared for Anything-Two things that you need to look for and be prepared for is for your airlock to become clogged or for foam to leak out of the airlock. By knowing about its potential for an appearance beforehand, so that you are not taken by surprise when it happens. TO help prepare for this is to place a large garbage bag under your primary fermenter and leave it open. That way the foam itself can leak cleanly into the bag instead of on your floor.

3. Don't Add More Yeast then you need-if you think that your batch is not fermenting, whatever you do don't add more yeast then you need. There

are two possible things that can happening during this time:

1. The fermentation process has not yet started and is taking longer than usual or 2. Your batch may be finished fermenting already. Yeast can start fermenting for at least 24-48 hours after you add it. So keep in mind that just because you don't see bubble in the airlock does not necessarily mean that fermenting isn't occurring. As long as the temperature is right, fermentation will occur regardless.

If you ever are in doubt or need to know for yourself if your batch is fermenting, use your hydrometer. A hydrometer will always let you know if fermentation is occur or has already occurred.

The Bottling Process and Some Helpful Tips

The bottling process is when your batch has finally finished fermenting and is ready for the last stage of completion before you can enjoy drinking it. When you place your batch into bottles you are preparing it for the aging stage where the brewing process is complete. Below are some helpful tips and trick to make the bottle process easier on you and some helpful tips on where you can get bottles for your beer for cheap.

1. Get bottles from your local bar-it is common knowledge that many bars and local pubs toss away any bottles they collect at the end of every night. To get bottles for free or for a discounted price, visit your local bar and simply ask them. You can even visit your local recycling center. The

bottles that you need to look for are not the screw cap type of bottles. However, the downside to getting free or discounted bottles from a bar or recycling center is that you need to wash and sanitize them thoroughly before your add your batch to them to reduce the risk of passing on harmful bacteria or harmful diseases.

Don't waste money on new bottles when you can easily ask your neighbors, friends, family or coworkers for their used bottles. You can even offer to give them a few free beers in exchange for reusing their bottles.

2. Remove the Label-Why would you want to fill bottles with your premium beer when another beer company's name is stamped on to it? There are numerous ways that you can remove these stubborn labels such as soaking the bottles in ammonia, soaking it in soap and water or steaming the labels to remove it. However, one of

the best ways to remove a label from a beer bottle is to soak the bottles in water that is mixed with 8 Tablespoon of Baking Soda for at least one hour minimum.

3. Use Only Brown Colored Beer Bottles-the worst beer bottles that you can use are both clear and brown beer bottles. The reason behind this is simple: green and clear bottles cause the light to affect the beer within it which can lead to a skunk like smell to occur.

4. Make large quantities of Beer-surprisingly, the larger amount of beer that you produce, the better the aging process turns out to be. The reason this happens is because the beer ages better when there is less exposure to oxygen. Try to use larger bottles such as 22 ounces rather than a 16 ounce bottle. However, if you are

planning to enter a beer competition, than you will have to only pour your batch into 12 ounce bottles.

5. Bottle Your Beer Carefully-one of the things that can happen is the horrible beer bomb. To avoid this happening make sure that you beer is fully fermented before bottling it, make sure that you measure your primary sugar precisely, and make sure that you mix it thoroughly to make sure that you have even carbonation throughout.

6. Make Sure That You Have Adequate Preparation the Day Before-the best time to prepare your beer for the bottling process, prepare your bottles the day before you actually need them. Place a small amount of water in each bottle the night before and let them air dry right before you need them. Also keep track of how

many bottle caps you are going to need beforehand so that you have everything you need when you begin to bottle your beer.

7. Condition Your Bottles Beforehand-many experienced homebrewers are anal about eliminating every tiny trace of sediment within their bottles. However, this is virtually impossible unless they have a key or they filter out their beer precisely. If you over-obsess with sediment in your bottles, you will never be happy with any batch you make. You will end up contaminating or oxidizing it too much. The key thing to do here is relax and just have fun making your own beer and do not over-obsess about the small things.

Conclusion

Homebrewing is one of those things that can be the most enjoyable hobby you can enjoy and you can reap great rewards from it. For many of us we simply enjoy the thought of consuming something that we made from scratch or we enjoy something that contains everything that we love.

However, for many people they stress over every little detail about homebrewing such as too much sediment in the bottles, whether the fermentation process is complete or incomplete, worrying about too much yeast in their batch and wanting every detail to be perfect. Homebrewing itself is something that requires you to make many mistakes and to learn from them in order to make your next batch better than the last.

When it comes to home brewing the key thing is to have fun and relax. It is something meant to help you relax and enjoy yourself, not to stress you out. You are supposed to make mistakes, you are supposed to learn this craft as you would with anything else and you are supposed to have fun. As long as you relax and enjoy yourself, I can definitely see you brewing your own beer from the comfort of your own home for many years to come.

About Us:

THE THOUGHT FLAME

TURNING SPARK INTO FLAME

The Thought Flame is committed to add value to its customers through various books, online courses and other resources. You can learn more about us and our books at www.thethoughtflame.com.

Don't forget to check out our amazing **online video courses** at www.thethoughtflame.com/courses/ to take your knowledge to another level.

To check out our **extraordinary collection of diet/cookbooks**, visit http://www.thethoughtflame.com/category/non-fictional/cookbooks/ .

As a part of our valued relationship with our customers, we keep providing you free promotional books, courses and other stuff on subscribing with us on our site. We have a strict anti-spam policy and assure you no spam mails will be sent to your mailbox.

To subscribe with us, visit

www.thethoughtflame.com.

Like our work and would like to say thanks?

Buy us a cup of coffee at

www.thethoughtflame.com/coffee/

Author:

Amarpreet Singh is an avid learner and his passion for education has made him travel, work and study all across the world. He holds three masters degrees, including MBA, from top universities in Asia.

He is author of dozens of books, many of which are Amazon's bestseller, varying in various topics and categories. He also teaches many online courses having thousands of students across the world.

He has a keen interest in international affairs, economics, global poverty and politics, financial markets and entrepreneurship, and strives to be part of a community that shares the same passion.

He has worked as consultant with organizations like Airbus and The World Bank.

He loves travelling and learning about new cultures, and has been fortunate to live/work/travel/study in countries like India, China, Korea, US, South Africa, Japan, Philippines, Singapore, Canada etc., and learn about the culture and lifestyle in each of them.

To check out more of his work, visit
www.thethoughtflame.com

12512958R00039

Printed in Great Britain
by Amazon